Robots Run Riot

Written by Jenny Feely

Illustrated by Alex Stitt

Flying Start
to Literacy®

Jodie had a farm. On her farm
she grew lots and lots of vegetables.

It was hard work growing vegetables,
but Jodie did not mind because
she had invented lots of robots
to help her with all the farm jobs.

These robots did all the things
that Jodie did not want to do.
They worked all day and did not stop
until sunset.

Jodie had four robots.

Slugbot was a robot that could catch the slugs that ate Jodie's vegetables.

Slugbot found all the slugs and then picked them up and dropped them into a tank.

Dogbot ran and barked at the cows.

All day long Dogbot made the cows go from paddock to paddock. At sunrise and sunset, Dogbot made the cows go to the milk shed to be milked.

Spraybot was a robot with wheels
and a large water tank. It could fill up
its tank from the dam and then
water the plants.

CLICK!

Eggbot was a robot with long, thin arms. All day long it gently collected the eggs from the chickens. Then it packed them into egg boxes, ready to sell.

It all worked very well.

Every night when the sun went down,
the robots went into the shed.
Jodie would hook them up
to the charger to get their batteries
recharged, ready for the next day.

But one night, while the robots were being recharged, there was a terrible storm.

All of a sudden, a big bolt of lightning hit the shed and sent a huge amount of electricity into the robots. This made the robots buzz in a very strange way.

Then another bolt of lightning hit the shed and, still buzzing, the robots rushed out of the shed and into the night.

Slugbot went into the chicken coop.
It picked up all the eggs and dropped
them into its holding tank.
Soon there were broken eggs everywhere.

Spraybot hurried off to fill up its tank.
But instead of going to the dam,
it went into the milk shed. It sucked up
all of the milk in the milk vats
and went out into the garden.
Soon it was spraying milk everywhere.

Eggbot went into the garden.
It picked up the slugs and put them
into the egg boxes. Soon all the
egg boxes were full – of slugs!

Dogbot ran into the chicken coop.
It barked and barked at the chickens
and chased them out of the chicken coop
and across the yard. It chased them
into the house, up the stairs
and into Jodie's bedroom.

Jodie woke up with a fright.
There were chickens everywhere.

"What are you doing?" yelled Jodie.

And then she noticed that Dogbot was buzzing in a funny way. Jodie reached over and pushed a button on Dogbot's nose.

Dogbot stopped buzzing and running and barking.

Jodie ran out of the house and found the other robots. She turned them off as quickly as she could.

And from that day on, Jodie always checked the weather forecast before she hooked up her robots to be recharged.